D1536687

Furniture Repairs from A to Z

A
Quick Reference Guide
of
Tips and Techniques

Donna S. Morris

Phoenix Press, Ltd.
La Verne, California

Library of Congress Cataloging in Publication Data

Morris, Donna S.
Furniture Repairs from A to Z – A Quick Reference Guide of
Tips and Techniques/ by/ Donna S. Morris
First Printing 2000

Includes index
1. Furniture - Repairing   2. Furniture finishing

Library of Congress Control Number: 00-091035

ISBN 0-9665673-4-X $14.95 Softcover

Phoenix Press, Ltd.
1407 Foothill Blvd., PMB 141
La Verne, California 91750

Manufactured and printed in the United States of America

The instructions in this book are not intended to be used for the restoration or repair of costly, "museum-quality" pieces. Rare or valuable furniture belongs in the hands of a qualified professional. Even a minor repair, improperly done, can have a major effect on the appraised value.

The contents of this book are intended as a guide, to be intelligently used. The restoration and repair methods have been described in detail, and precautions in handling the various chemicals that are potentially hazardous if improperly used have been explicitly pointed out. Every effort has been made to make this book as complete and accurate as possible. All instructions and precautions should be carefully followed. Because the actual use of the methods and materials described in this book are entirely in the hands of the reader, neither the author, nor the publisher, can guarantee the results of any instructions or formulas, and therefore each of them expressly disclaims any responsibility for injury to persons or property through their use.

If you do not wish to be bound by the above, you may return this book to the publisher for a full refund.

Acknowledgments

I would like to extend my gratitude once again to all of the students, clients and friends who have contributed to this book. Their questions, problems and furniture have helped me accumulate this eclectic collection of tips and techniques.

Special thanks to my mother, Hazel, and to Carmen and Larry for their love and support of my latest "baby". To Sharon, Helené, Jason and Buzz because they keep believing. To Kevin who once again went above and beyond the call of duty with his patience and computer knowledge. To Steve Chandler for his help with the cover. To Paul, my Panamanian amigo, David and Carolyn Long and The College for Appraisers, and Sue Hopkins and *The Jumble*. Very special thanks to Frank Donadee and *The Collector* for planting the seeds for this book.

Dedicated to the memory of my father
Donald S. Betts

Furniture repair tips and tricks are useless!

... unless you can remember them (or remember where to find them) when you need them. The following pages contain a variety of tips and techniques to make furniture repairs easier and less expensive. They have been arranged alphabetically so you don't have to search for them when you need them and you don't have to remember them. You just have to remember where you put this book!

Most of the tips can be done using items you currently have in your home. Some are so simple they require little more than your hands. Others are downright quirky and "off the wall". But they all work!

Foreword

This new book of Donna's is going to raise a lot of controversy within two special interests, namely the community of professional restorers and those who sell the myriad of products relating to refinishing, restoring and cleaning of furniture. Her book strips away much of the mystery that has prevented the average person who finds a table at a garage sale from making minor improvements. The products that she recommends are not the exotic, expensive kinds of items that you may need once or twice a decade, but the things that you may easily find in your refrigerator or kitchen cabinet. Because of the simple, straight forward approach taken, the novice will have no trouble following the steps presented. This book does the two things critically needed in the saving of antiques. First, it makes the information readily available to the end user. Second, it makes the means to accomplish the task within the reach of everyone.

Frank Donadee
Southern California Collector's Association

ADHESIVES (removing from a finish)
Rub the adhesive with creamy peanut butter, cold cream or salad oil. Allow to sit for a few minutes, then wipe off with a soft cloth. Stubborn spots can be coaxed off by lightly scraping with the edge of a plastic credit card.

ALCOHOL (rubbing alcohol) for shining chrome
Dampen a soft cloth with rubbing alcohol and buff chrome surfaces. Follow by buffing with a dry cloth.

ALCOHOL (rubbing alcohol) for surface preparation
A soft cloth dampened with rubbing alcohol can be used to clean sanding dust, etc. from a sanded surface before applying a coat of stain or finish.

ALCOHOL STAINS (removing from a finish)
Apply a small amount of cream silver polish to your finger and gently rub over the white spot. When the stain is gone,

wipe off any surface grit from the polish, then apply a coat of wax or furniture polish.

ALUM POWDER (for cleaning aluminum)

Mix 1 tablespoon of alum powder and 1 tablespoon of cornstarch together in a bowl with enough water to form a stiff paste. Use a damp sponge or rag to apply to aluminum to remove stains and discolorations. Let the paste dry completely, then rinse with hot water and dry with a soft cloth.

ALUMINUM FOIL (to clean and polish aluminum)

Aluminum furniture can be polished by rubbing with a wadded-up piece of aluminum foil. Rust spots and other stubborn stains can often be removed by rubbing with a wadded-up piece of aluminum foil dipped in cola. Rinse thoroughly and dry to prevent water spots.

ALUMINUM FOIL (to patch small worn spots on mirrors)

Tape a small piece of aluminum foil on the reflective backing of a mirror to help disguise small age spots in the mirror.

ALUMINUM FOIL (to retard stripper)

Apply furniture stripper or remover to furniture, then cover with a piece of aluminum foil to increase its effectiveness and retard evaporation.

ALUMINUM FURNITURE (cleaning)

Mix a mild solution of dishwashing liquid and hot water. Use a sponge or soft brush to apply solution and remove dirt and grime. Rinse well then dry thoroughly to prevent water spots. Baking soda makes a good non-abrasive cleaner for removing stubborn spots. Apply baking soda with a damp cloth. Rub the soiled area until clean, then rinse well and dry. Stubborn grime can also be removed by rubbing with a piece of 4/0 steel wool dipped in kerosene.

ALUMINUM FURNITURE (cleaning)

Put 2 tablespoons of cream of tartar in a small bowl. Add white vinegar, a little at a time, until you have a stiff paste. If it should become too liquid, add a little more cream of tartar. Use a sponge or a soft cloth to rub the resulting paste on aluminum to remove stains and discolorations. Let the paste dry completely before washing it off with hot water. Rub dry with a clean cloth.

ALUMINUM FURNITURE (polishing)

Rub aluminum furniture with the cut part of a fresh lemon to polish and bring back the shine. Buff dry with a soft cloth.

ALUMINUM FURNITURE (protecting)

Apply a light coat of car wax to the furniture and allow it to dry until a haze forms. Then buff to remove excess wax.

BABY OIL (to remove paper stuck to a finish)
Cover the paper with a thin coat of baby oil. Let the oil soak into the paper. Then rub the paper off with a soft cloth. *Never* use metal knives or scrapers to remove paper stuck to a furniture finish as they can permanently damage the finish or dent the wood. Stubborn spots can be coaxed off by using the edge of a plastic credit card.

BABY OIL (to remove white spots from a finish)
Dip your finger into the baby oil then into some cigarette ashes. Lightly rub your finger over the white area. Stop frequently to check your progress and do not use excessive pressure. When the white mark is removed, wipe off any remaining oil and ashes.

BABY POWDER (to buff and polish marble)
Sprinkle baby powder on the marble surface. Use a clean chalk board eraser or soft cloth to buff marble to a soft gleam. Use a clean cloth to remove any excess powder.

BABY WIPES (for coffee spills on upholstery)
Blot spilled coffee with a baby wipe to absorb the coffee before it leaves a stain.

BAKING SODA (for cleaning stainless steel and aluminum)
Apply baking soda to the furniture with a damp cloth. Lightly rub the soiled area until clean. Rinse well with clean water and dry thoroughly to prevent water spots.

BAKING SODA (to remove odors from upholstered furniture)
Liberally sprinkle baking soda on the upholstery. Wait an hour or more, then vacuum.

BAMBOO FURNITURE (cleaning)
Clean bamboo furniture with a slightly dampened cloth. Dry thoroughly. An occasional coat of natural-based wax will help prevent marks and stains and maintain the original luster. Apply wax sparingly. Allow to dry to a haze, then buff.

BAMBOO POLES
Old bamboo poles can be cut into small pieces with a utility knife and shaped into custom stripping tools. The bamboo is soft enough that it will not scratch or mar most woods but strong enough to help remove built-up finish and gunk.

BEER (removing stains from upholstery)

Dried beer stains can be removed from upholstery by sponging the stain with a solution of 1 part white vinegar and 1 part water. Do not over-saturate the fabric. Blot with a white towel and allow to air dry.

BEER (stale)

Dampen a soft cloth with stale beer and lightly rub leather furniture to clean off dirt and grime. Wipe with a cloth slightly dampened in water to rinse. Lightly buff dry.

BEER (warm)

Dip a soft cloth into warm beer. Wring out excess. Use to dust waxed oak, mahogany, walnut and pine furniture.

BEESWAX (to fill fine cracks in wood)

Rub a cake of beeswax over the cracks rubbing both with the crack and across the crack. Buff off excess wax with a soft cloth.

BICYCLING GLOVES

Hammers and screwdrivers can be very hard on your hand muscles. To cushion your hand, wear an old bicycling glove. The gloves are fingerless so you can still pick up nails, screws and tools, but the padded palm will cushion your hand.

BLACK LACQUER FURNITURE (cleaning)

Dip a soft cloth into strong-brewed tea. Lightly wipe the furniture and buff dry with a separate cloth.

BLOOD (removing stains from marble)

Mix a mild solution of TSP and water. Use a soft cloth or cotton swabs to apply the solution to the stain. Allow to sit for a few minutes. Then wipe off any remaining solution and rinse the area by wiping with a damp cloth. Dry thoroughly.

BLOOD (removing stains from upholstery fabric)

Cover the stain as soon as possible with a paste made from cornstarch and water. Rub the paste lightly into the fabric. Then place the furniture in the sun, if possible, to dry the paste and draw the blood out into the cornstarch. When dry, brush off the powder. Repeat the process if necessary.

BOBBY PINS

If the nail, screw or brad you are trying to drive into the wood is too small to hold with your fingers, use a bobby pin to hold it in place.

BRASS (cleaning)

Place brass hardware in a dish or glass jar and cover with full strength household ammonia. Soak the pieces for 10 to 15 minutes. Stubborn pieces may need to be scrubbed with an old toothbrush or a small piece of 4/0 steel wool. Rinse the brass with water and dry thoroughly.

An alternative method: Mix equal parts of flour and salt. Add enough white vinegar to make a paste. Spread a thick layer of the paste on the brass and allow to dry. Wash off the dry paste and rinse clean. Dry thoroughly.

BRASS (identifying solid)
A simple magnet will easily help you to identify solid brass. Brass is not magnetic and steel is. A magnet will not stick to solid brass but will stick to brass-plated metal.

BREAD
Surface dirt can be removed from sueded leather furniture by lightly rubbing the suede with slices of white bread. After the stains are removed, lightly brush with a suede brush to restore the nap.

BROOMSTICK (or piece of dowel for sanding block)
Glue a piece of felt or foam rubber around a piece of broomstick or old dowel. Wrap sandpaper over it and use to sand curved areas. Especially good for smoothing inward curves.

BURLAP

Cut a piece of burlap and twist it to resemble a rope. Use to rub wood to help remove stubborn paint and finish that has been softened by stripper or remover. For rounded legs etc. hold one end in each hand and pull back and forth around the leg as you would a shoe shine rag.

BUTCHER BLOCK TABLES (degreasing)

Pour white vinegar onto the butcher block table top. Use a clean sponge to scrub the surface. Rinse with water, then dry thoroughly.

BUTCHER BLOCK TABLES (deodorizing)

Sprinkle baking soda on the butcher block table top. Use a damp sponge to scrub the baking soda into the wood. Rinse well with water and dry thoroughly.

BUTCHER BLOCK TABLES (disinfecting)

Mix 2 or 3 tablespoons of laundry bleach to one quart of water. Apply to the table top with a clean sponge or cloth. Rinse by wiping with a cloth dipped in water. Dry thoroughly.

BUTCHER BLOCK TABLES (redressing)

Thoroughly scrape and clean the table prior to redressing. Use only oils with FDA approved ingredients for use on butcher blocks. Do not use vegetable oil. It will provide minimal protection and will turn sticky and may become rancid. Apply oil liberally with a soft cloth. Allow the oil to penetrate into the wood surface, then wipe off excess with a clean cloth. Buff with a soft cloth to work the oil into the wood pores.

BUTCHER BLOCK TABLES (removing stains)
Soak a white cloth or white paper towels with laundry bleach. Place over the stained area. Allow it to sit on the stain for at least 15 minutes. Remove the towel and rinse the area with a clean cloth dampened with water. Dry thoroughly.

BUTCHER BLOCK TABLES (removing wax and gum)
Put several ice cubes in a plastic sandwich baggie. Apply the ice pack to the wax or gum. Allow to remain until the wax or gum becomes brittle. Then use the edge of a plastic credit card, or a plastic scraper to remove it. Always scrape with the grain to avoid damaging the wood surface.

CANE (repairing a sagging cane seat)

Turn the chair upside down to expose the rough underside of the cane. Mix 1-1/2 oz. of glycerin into 1 pint of water. Sponge the solution on the cane. Allow to penetrate for a few minutes until the cane is well soaked. Use clean rags or white paper towels to mop off excess solution. Turn the chair upright and allow to dry away from direct sources of heat or sunlight.

CHROME FURNITURE (cleaning)

For general cleaning, wash chrome with a mild solution of dishwashing liquid and water. Rinse and dry thoroughly. For stubborn grime dip a sponge into cider vinegar and rub. Rinse with water and buff dry. Some stains may be removed from chrome by rubbing with a soft cloth dipped in baby oil. After the stain is removed, buff with a soft cloth to remove excess oil.

CAN OPENER

Use a "church key" style can opener as a stripping tool. The pointed end is perfect for cleaning out grooves and carving.

CANVAS SEATS (cleaning)

Canvas seats and chair backs should be removed from the furniture prior to cleaning and placed on a firm, non-absorbent surface. Mix a mild solution of dishwashing liquid and water and use a sponge or soft scrub brush to remove accumulated dirt. Rinse thoroughly with cold water. Return the canvas pieces to the chair frame while they are still wet. Allow to air dry away from direct sunlight.

CAR WAX

See: FORMICA brand laminate FURNITURE TOPS AND PLASTIC FURNITURE (rejuvenating a dull finish)

Do not use car wax on wooden furniture! It will build up and ruin the finish and is not removable.

CASTERS (repairing loose)

A temporary repair can be made by wrapping a small piece of steel wool or plastic tape around the socket of the caster to give it a tighter fit in the hole in the furniture.

CASTOR OIL (for reviving leather)

Combine 2 parts denatured alcohol and 3 parts castor oil. Use a soft cloth to lightly rub the mixture into a clean leather surface until it is absorbed. Allow to sit for 24-48 hours, then apply a light coat of castor oil alone. Rub the castor oil into the leather until it is absorbed.

CATSUP (for cleaning brass)

Pour a generous amount of catsup on a clean sponge and rub onto the brass pieces. Allow them to sit for at least an hour (longer if they are badly tarnished). Really badly tarnished items may need to soak overnight. Rinse with hot water and soap. Dry thoroughly.

CEDAR CHESTS (restoring cedar smell)

Lightly sand the unfinished interior wood with fine sandpaper to expose new wood and release cedar oil. Wipe sawdust off with a soft cloth or vacuum thoroughly before re-use.

CHALK (for repairing marble)

Crush the chalk into a powder. Dip a slightly dampened chamois or thick rag into the chalk. Rub in circles over the ring or stain in the marble surface. When the surface feels smooth, rinse the area with clear water. Blot dry then allow to air dry.

CHALK (to clean vinyl)

Grind up enough pieces of chalk to make 1/3 cup. Mix with 1 cup of baking soda. Sprinkle the mixture on a dampened sponge or old washcloth and scrub the vinyl. Rinse with clear water and dry thoroughly to prevent water spots.

CHALK (to prevent a screwdriver from slipping)
Apply chalk to the end of the screwdriver blade before inserting into the screwhead to help prevent the screwdriver from slipping out of the groove.

CHALK
See: TOOLS (preventing rust)

CHOCOLATE (removing stains from upholstery)
Use a soft cloth to lightly rub glycerin into the spot. Dampen a cloth with clear water and blot the stain. It may be necessary to repeat the process to remove stubborn stains.

CHOP STICKS
Use chop sticks to clean out the sliding parts on the tracks of metal table extension mechanisms.

CHROME FURNITURE (polishing)
Apply a small dab of conditioning hair gel (like Alberto VO5 Conditioning Hairdressing) to a soft cloth. Rub the cloth over the chrome, then use a clean, soft cloth to buff off the excess.

CHROME FURNITURE (removing stains)
Dampen a soft cloth with baby oil and rub the stained area.

Use a clean soft cloth to buff and polish the chrome dry.

CIDER VINEGAR

Saturate a sponge or a clean cloth with cider vinegar. Rub on chrome to clean and degrease. Rinse with warm water. Dry thoroughly to prevent water spots.

CIGARETTE BURNS (removing)

Lightly scrape away any damaged finish with a single edged razor blade. Touch up the color of the wood with wood stain, if necessary. Use clear nail polish to touch-up the finish.

CLUB SODA (removing stains from upholstery)

Apply club soda to the stain with a sponge or soft white cloth. Do not use colored sponges or cloths as they may transfer color to the upholstery and create another stain. Rub small amounts of club soda into the stain until the stain is lifted. Blot with white towels and allow to air dry.

CLUB SODA

(See: RUSTY NUTS, BOLTS AND SCREWS, loosening)

COFFEE (instant)
Instant coffee can be mixed into spackling paste or wood filler to help achieve the proper woodtone.

COFFEE (instant)
See: SCRATCHES, removing from dark wood

COFFEE FILTERS
Use coffee filters for a lint-free way to wipe clean mirrors and glass table tops. They also work well for cleaning plexiglass without scratching the surface.

COLD CREAM (for removing adhesive from a finish)
Rub cold cream on the adhesive spot. Allow to sit for a few minutes. Then wipe off with a soft cloth. Any stubborn adhesive spots can be removed by lightly scraping , with the grain, with a plastic credit card.

COMB
Place small nails or tacks between the teeth of a comb. The comb will hold the nails or tacks securely and your fingers will not be in the way of the hammer.

COMPOSITION-WOOD FURNITURE (cleaning)

Do not use water to clean composition-wood furniture. Use only soft dry cloths. Grease, ink and stubborn stains can be removed by rubbing the area with a soft cloth dampened with a small amount of paint thinner. Small scratches in the finish can often be removed by rubbing with a vinyl protectant product such as "ARMOR ALL". Apply a small amount to a soft cloth and lightly rub over the scratch.

CORKS (drilling guide)

If you need to drill more than one hole of the same depth in order to do a furniture repair, place a cork on the drill bit just above the depth you will need. When the cork makes contact with the surface, you will know the hole is the right depth.

CORKS (polishing brass)

Small unlacquered pieces of brass hardware can be polished by rubbing with a piece of cork.

CORN STARCH (cleaning wood, especially good for cleaning "whitewashed wood")

Mix together 1 cup of warm water and 2 teaspoons of corn-starch in an empty spray bottle. Shake until the ingredients are thoroughly mixed. Lightly spray the solution on the wood and allow it to dry. Wipe off with a soft clean rag.

CORN STARCH
See: FURNITURE POLISH, removing excess

CRAYONS (to repair dents in wood)
Pick a crayon that closely matches the color of the wood. Rub the crayon over the dent to fill. Then use the edge of a plastic credit card to remove the excess and level the repair with the surface of the wood. Lightly buff the repair with a soft cloth to blend edges.

DECALS (removing from furniture)
Cover the decal with white vinegar. Apply pieces of cloth or white paper towel if necessary to keep the decal moist. Allow the vinegar to soak into the decal, then rub with a soft cloth to remove. Stubborn spots can be coaxed off by scraping with the edge of a plastic credit card. Wipe the area with a damp cloth and dry thoroughly after the decal has been removed.

DENTAL FLOSS
Use dental floss to remove paint or finishes from grooves

carved in legs, etc. Cut a piece at least 12" long. Hold the end of a piece of unwaxed dental floss in each hand. Place the dental floss in the groove and pull it back and forth. Change pieces of dental floss as necessary.

DENTS (filling dents in wood)
Position the furniture so that the dent is on a horizontal surface. Use a fine sewing needle to prick several holes into the wood. Make the holes in the wood grain if possible. Use the tip of your finger or an eye dropper to fill the dent with water. Allow the water to penetrate. The water will expand the wood fibers and raise the dent. Some dents may require multiple applications. When the dent has risen, wipe off the excess water.

"DO -IT-YOURSELF" DUSTING CLOTHS
You can make "do-it-yourself" dusting cloths that work as well as the store bought ones ... with the added bonus that they contain no silicones! Mix 1/2 teaspoon of olive oil and 1/4 cup of vinegar (or lemon juice) in a small bowl. Saturate a soft lint-free cloth in the solution. Wring out and shake to remove excess moisture. Use the treated cloth to dust, polish and shine your furniture. The dust rag can be reused over and over. When it becomes dirty, rinse under hot running water, wring out and remoisten with the solution.

DOORS
A tip to prevent the need for a repair: If your bookcase, armoire

or china cabinet has an interior catch, make sure it is locked before closing the second door. This will prevent the doors from accidentally opening and splitting the wood around the lock if the piece is moved or bumped.

DOWELS
Before making a furniture repair with a dowel, take a pair of pliers and close them around the dowel. Then pull them lengthwise down the dowel to create a series of grooves. These grooves will hold the glue as the dowel is inserted into the hole and you will get a better glue bond and a more successful repair.

DRAWERS (repairing sticking metal slides)
Remove the drawer. Lubricate the slides with a small amount of grease, oil, or conditioning hair gel.

DRAWERS (repairing sticking wooden runners)
Remove the drawer. Lightly sand the drawer runners with sandpaper or an emeryboard. Then lubricate them by rubbing with paraffin, a candle or a bar of soap.

DUST CLOTHS
Add 2 teaspoons of turpentine to a quart of hot sudsy water

and mix together. Add several lint-free cloths and allow to soak overnight. Wring out the cloths and allow to dry. The cloths will attract dust like "store bought treated cloths".

EGGS (to remove grease spots and difficult stains from leather)
Separate an egg. Beat the egg white until stiff. Use a soft cloth to apply the stiffened egg white to the leather. Rub lightly until the stain is gone.

EMERY BOARDS
Emery boards can be used in lieu of sandpaper for small repairs on wooden furniture.

ERASERS
Store small drill bits by screwing the ends point first, into an eraser. The bits will be easier to find and the points will not rust or corrode.

ERASERS

Use a Pink Pearl Eraser to remove soil from cotton upholstery. Lightly rub the soil with the eraser, then brush to remove eraser dust.

EYEBROW PENCIL (to cover scratches in dark wood)

Scratches in ebony wood, and some dark walnut and dark oak pieces can be covered by rubbing an eyebrow pencil over the scratch. Buff with a soft cloth afterwards to blend the repair.

FABRIC SOFTENER (for cleaning glass and plexiglass)

Mix a capful of liquid fabric softener in a quart of water. Use a lintfree cloth to wipe the mixture sparingly onto glass or plexiglass. Then buff dry with another lintfree cloth.

FABRIC SOFTENER SHEETS (to polish chrome)

Slightly dampen a fabric softener sheet and rub it on chrome furniture to polish and shine it.

FABRIC SOFTENER SHEETS (to remove dust after sanding)

Fabric softener sheets can be used in lieu of a tack rag. Wipe wooden furniture with a fabric softener sheet to remove excess sanding dust before applying a finish.

FABRIC SOFTENER SHEETS (to remove pet hair)

Lightly rub a fabric softener sheet over upholstered furniture. It will collect and remove pet hair and help remove pet odors.

FELT TIP MARKERS

Use a black felt tip marker to touch up wrought iron furniture. Apply a small amount of wax over the repair to seal it.

FILM CONTAINERS

Place the lids from empty 35 mm film containers on the ends of clamps to protect the wood from clamp damage.

FLYSPECKING

To simulate flyspecking, dip a toothbrush in black paint and rub it against a piece of wire screening held over the piece of furniture.

FORMICA ® brand laminate FURNITURE TOPS (cleaning)

Squeeze a small amount of suntan lotion on a soft cloth. Rub greasy dirty areas, then buff with a clean cloth.

FORMICA ® brand laminate FURNITURE TOPS (rejuvenating a dull finish)

Apply a small amount of liquid car wax to a soft cloth and rub over the dull finish. Allow to set until the wax forms a dull haze. Then buff with a clean cloth.

This process will also rejuvenate plastic furniture.

FORMICA ® brand laminate FURNITURE TOPS (removing stains)

Coffee, tea and other stubborn stains can usually be removed with a simple paste made of baking soda and water. Apply the paste to the stained area, and allow to sit for approximately 15 minutes. Rinse with water, then dry the surface. For more difficult stains use a mixture of equal parts of water and laundry bleach. Apply solution to the stained area. Rinse immediately with water and dry. Lemon juice can also be used to remove many stubborn stains. Apply lemon juice to the stain, then rinse with water and dry when the stain is removed.

FURNITURE POLISH (removing excess)

If you have applied too much furniture polish and can not

wipe off all of the excess, sprinkle a little corn starch over the polish then wipe off with a soft cloth.

GARDEN HOSE

Cut a small piece of garden hose. Cut a slit completely down one side. Tuck one edge of a piece of sandpaper into the slit and wrap the paper around the hose for a flexible sanding block useful for sanding curves.

GESSO (reconstructing)

Mix together 1/2 teaspoon of plaster of Paris, a small amount of water and a small amount of white glue in a shot glass or other small container. Use a small piece of wood to mix the ingredients. The mixture will begin to set quickly – usually within 3 minutes – so you will want to mix small amounts and work fast. Remove the gesso from the glass and work into a ball with your fingers. Shape the gesso to conform to the shape of the missing decorative pieces. Allow to dry overnight. When dry, lightly sand with an emeryboard. Remove any dust. Then finish to match the surround areas.

GLASS (cleaning)

Dissolve 1/4 cup dishwasher detergent in 1 gallon of very hot water. Scrub glass with soft cloth, then wipe clean with a dry cloth. (Most dishwasher detergents contain water softening agents so the finish will be shiny and spot free without rinsing.)

GLASS TABLE TOPS (removing minor scratches)

Dampen your finger (or a soft cloth) with water and apply a small amount of "tooth whitening" toothpaste (not the gel kind). Lightly rub the scratched glass surface. Wipe off toothpaste with a clean cloth moistened with water. Dry thoroughly.

GLUE (removing from furniture)

Airplane glue or other "cement" type glues can be removed from furniture by rubbing with cold cream or salad oil. Use your finger or a soft cloth to apply, then rub off with a soft cloth.

GOLD LEAF (cleaning)

Mix together 1/2 cup denatured alcohol and 1 cup of water. Dampen a soft cloth with the mixture and lightly wipe over the area. Blot dry immediately with a soft cloth.

GREASE STAINS ON UPHOLSTERY FABRIC (removing)

Liberally sprinkle the grease stain with baking soda. Allow to sit on the stain for at least an hour. Then vacuum to remove. Additional applications may be required.

GREASE STAINS IN WOOD (removing)

Some grease stains can be removed by wiping the stained area with a cloth moistened with paint thinner. Others may be removed by wiping with a cloth dampened with alcohol. Stubborn grease stains can often be removed by covering the stain with rug cleaner containing a base of wood flour and trichlorethylene. Allow the cleaner to dry, then brush away the dust.

HAIR DRYER (to clean inlay)

Use a hair dryer set on the "cool" or "no heat" setting to clean inlaid surfaces and boulle (marquetry that uses very thin sheets of mother-of-pearl, ivory, tortoiseshell, brass or pewter). Do not use a dust cloth or a chamois to clean inlay. Loose pieces can be pulled out of place if they catch on the cloth fibers or leather.

HAIR DRYER (to loosen screws)
Set the hair dryer to the lowest setting. Use a back and forth motion to apply heat to the area that contains the stubborn screw. After a few minutes the screw should come out easily.

HAIR SPRAY
Apply a light coat of hair spray to polished brass or copper to prevent tarnish.

HANDS
The heat of your hand can help remove the stain from an alcohol spill. Use clean cloths to mop up the liquid immediately after the spill, then rub the area with your hand. The oil and heat of your hand will help to restore some of the oil removed from the wood by the alcohol.

HIGH CHAIRS (cleaning)
The chrome and vinyl components of high chairs can be safely cleaned by wiping with a damp sponge dipped in baking soda. Rinse with a damp cloth and dry.

HINGES (not closing properly)
Hinges have a tendency to loosen with use and age. If the problem is left unchecked, the doors will eventually not close properly. Remove the hinge pin. Tap a slight bend in the center of it, and then replace it. This will usually help the hinge open and close more smoothly.

HINGES (sticking)

Put a small dab of conditioning hair treatment (like Alberto VO5 Conditioning Hairdressing) on your finger and rub it into the sticky hinge. It is less messy than oil and will not run all over the furniture.

HOLES IN THE WOOD (filling)

Small tack holes or nail holes in wood can be filled by dipping a wooden toothpick into wood glue and inserting the toothpick into the hole. Use a single edge razor blade to trim the toothpick so that it is flush with the finish. Lightly sand smooth if necessary and finish to match surrounding wood.

HYDROGEN PEROXIDE (to remove stains from marble)

Do not use on colored marble. Dip a cotton swab into 35% solution of hydrogen peroxide. Lightly rub over the stained area. When the stain is removed, wipe with another swab dampened with clear water. Blot dry, then allow to air dry.

ICE (to remove wax and gum from upholstery fabric)

Put an ice cube in a plastic sandwich baggie or a piece of plastic wrap and hold it against the wax or gum until it freezes.

After it is frozen hard, use the edge of a credit card to scrape it off.

INK (removing stains from leather)
Some ink stains can be removed from leather by brushing the stain with skim milk. Allow the milk to penetrate the stain. Then polish the leather with a soft dry cloth to work out the ink.

INK (removing stains from marble)
For minor stains, crush a piece of chalk to make a powder or use pumice, and lightly rub on the stain in a circular motion with a slightly dampened soft cloth. When the stain is removed, rinse off the powder with water and blot dry.

An alternative method: Dip a cotton swab into laundry bleach or hydrogen peroxide. Carefully apply to the ink stain. Blot off excess bleaching agent and rinse by wiping with a clean cloth dampened with water. Blot dry.

INK (removing stains from vinyl)
Spray the ink with hairspray, then blot until the stain is removed. Rinse with water and dry.

IODINE (to repair scratches in wood)
Carefully apply iodine to the scratch with a small brush. Avoid

getting iodine anywhere except the scratch. Keep a cloth or paper towel handy to wipe off any excess.

Old iodine turns dark brown with age and works very well for repairing dark walnut and mahogany.

Scratches in maple wood can be repaired with a solution of 50% iodine and 50% denatured alcohol.

JELL-O
Black cherry and cherry flavored Jell-o can be used to touch-up scratches in some red colored woods. Sprinkle a small amount of Jell-o powder into a dish and add just enough water to make a syrupy consistency. Use a small artist's brush to apply to the scratched area.

JOINTS (gluing)
Apply masking tape to the adjacent surfaces to prevent glue from squeezing out and staining the area around a joint. Carefully pull off the tape after the glue has dried.

JOINTS (repairing loose joints)

Some loose furniture joints can be successfully repaired by swelling the wood with water. Use an eye dropper (or your finger) to apply water to the loose joint. Be careful not to get excess water on the surrounding finish so as not to create a water mark. Allow the water to penetrate. Wipe off any excess. This process may have to be repeated several times.

JOINTS (sanding mitered corners and joints)

Place a piece of masking tape diagonally along the mitered edge of a corner, or on the wood of a joint when sanding to prevent sanding across the grain on different pieces of wood. Carefully remove the tape when the repair is completed.

KEROSENE

Apply a small amount of kerosene to a 3/0 steel wool pad and rub wrought iron furniture to clean the furniture, and remove rust. Change pads as needed. Coat the clean furniture with wax to prevent further rust and make the next cleaning easier.

KEYS (broken in lock)
Insert a coping saw blade into the keyhole just above the key's teeth. Hook the sawblade onto the front of the key shaft and pull it out.

KEYS (sticking in locks)
Spray the key with non-stick vegetable spray if aerosol graphite sprays aren't available to prevent it from sticking in the lock.

LACQUER (removing from brass hardware)
Use an old pot. Put the hardware in the pot. Add 6 tablespoons of baking soda for every quart of water. Fill the pot no more than half full. Bring the water to a boil. Allow to boil for approximately 30 minutes. Pour off the slimy liquid. Allow the hardware to cool. Then lightly rub out the brass with steel wool to loosen any remaining flakes of finish.

LATEX PAINT (removing from hands)

Stubborn latex paint can be quickly removed from your hands by squirting a small amount of shaving cream into your hands and then rubbing them together. Rinse with water.

LAUNDRY BLEACH (for removing black water marks from wood)

Use a swab or small paint brush to apply laundry bleach to the black water mark. Be careful to keep the bleach on the stain and off of the surrounding wood. Allow the bleach to penetrate. After the stain has been removed, wipe off excess bleach with white paper towels or clean rags. Then neutralize the area by wiping with white paper towels or white rags moistened with white vinegar. Follow up by wiping with water, then dry the area thoroughly.

LEATHER (cleaning)
(See: BEER , stale)

LEATHER (removing grease stains)

Separate an egg and beat the egg white until stiff. Use a soft cloth to apply the stiffened egg white to the grease spot. Rub lightly until the grease is gone.

LEATHER (removing indention marks)

Heavy objects can leave indentions in a leather surface. These can often be removed by applying lemon oil to the area twice a day for a week. This is usually sufficient amount of time to remoisten the leather and swell the fibers back to their original shape. A monthly application of leather conditioner will protect the leather and help prevent further dents from occurring.

LEATHER (removing mildew)

Wipe leather with a solution of equal parts of alcohol and water to kill mildew on the leather surface. Apply sparingly and do not over-wet the leather. Allow to dry away from direct sources of heat or sunlight.

LEATHER (removing wax from)

Wax build-up can be removed from leather with a solution of 1/4 cup white vinegar and 1/2 cup water. Dip a soft rag into the solution and wring out the rag to remove the excess solution. Carefully wipe the leather. Be careful not to saturate the leather. Remoisten and wring out the cloth often to avoid re-depositing the wax. Carefully blot the leather dry. *Do not* rub.

LEATHER (removing white rings)

White rings and other water marks left on the leather from water spills and condensation can be removed by covering the spot with petroleum jelly, then allowing it to remain for a day or two. Buff the remaining petroleum jelly off with a soft cloth.

LEATHER (repairing alcohol stains)

Alcohol stains can be caused by anything containing alcohol, (i.e. : perfumes and medicine as well as alcoholic beverages). Alcohol stains will usually bleach the color from the leather surface and will often leave a white mark. This is especially common on leather tops. Moisten saddle soap with a soft cloth and work up a good lather. Lightly rub on the leather working on a small area at a time. Wipe off the saddle soap with a clean dry cloth. Apply a second coat of saddle soap and allow to dry. Buff the leather with a dry cloth. If a lighter mark still remains, apply a scuff-proof type of shoe polish to the stained area and lightly feather the edges to blend the repair.

LEATHER TRUNKS (cleaning)

The leather on old trunks can be extremely thin, and extra care should be taken when cleaning them. Moisten a soft cloth with warm water and rub across saddle soap to work up a good lather. Gently rub the leather, working on a small area at a time. When the dirt has been removed, wipe off excess saddle soap with a clean dry cloth. Apply a second coat of saddle soap and allow to dry. Buff the leather with a dry cloth.

LEMON (for removing mildew from upholstery)

Cut a fresh lemon in half. Dip half the lemon into some salt and rub the mildew spots. Allow to dry. Place the furniture in the sun if possible. Brush off the mildew with a soft brush. You may want to follow-up this treatment with an application of upholstery shampoo.

LEMON JUICE (to polish aluminum)
Rub aluminum with a cut piece of fresh lemon. Buff dry with a soft cloth.

LEMON JUICE (to remove stains from a wood finish)
Use a small paint brush or a cotton swab to apply fresh lemon juice to an ink stain or other stubborn stain. After the stain is removed, use a white cloth or white paper towels dampened with water to remove the excess lemon juice. Blot the surface dry. The process may need to be repeated several times for older or more stubborn stains.

LIME REMOVER
Lime remover (the commercial kind that removes lime deposits and soap scum) works well for removing stubborn black tarnish from old brass. Apply it with a piece of 3/0 steel wool. Rub well, then rinse in hot water.

LIP BALM
Coat nails and screws with lip balm before inserting and they will penetrate wood more easily.

LOCKS (opening a locked lock)

These 2 "credit card tricks" will often help open old locks if the key is missing. Try sliding an old credit card between the locked door or drawer and the frame to press the latch into the door. If that doesn't work, try cutting an old credit card into an "L" shape, insert it between the door or drawer and the frame and pull it towards you to pop the lock open.

LOUVERED CABINET DOORS (cleaning)

The easiest way to clean the louvered cabinet doors on your furniture is with a new, soft paint brush slightly dampened with water. Start at the top of the door and methodically work your way to the bottom of the door.

MARBLE (cleaning)

Mix 1/2 cup of white vinegar, 1 cup of household ammonia, and 1/4 cup of baking soda into 1 gallon of water. Use a sponge or soft cloth to apply the solution to the marble. Lightly rub to remove grease, dirt and grime. Rinse with clear water and dry thoroughly.

MARBLE (moving)

Lift and carry large marble furniture components in a vertical position to prevent them from breaking under their own weight.

MARBLE (removing fine scratches)

Mix baking soda and water together to form a paste. Use extra fine steel wool to apply the paste to the scratched marble. Use light pressure and rub in small circles. Rinse off the paste by wiping with a soft cloth dampened in water. Dry thoroughly. Repeat the process if necessary.

MARBLE (removing greasy stains)

Dampen a small piece of blotting paper or a small piece of a coffee filter with denatured alcohol or acetone. Place the paper over the stain and then cover with a piece of plastic wrap. Wait about 30 minutes, then check on the stain. It may be necessary to repeat the process several times for older or more stubborn stains.

MARBLE (removing wine stains)

Use a cotton swab to apply 20% hydrogen peroxide solution to the stain. Allow to penetrate the stain, then wipe off with a soft cloth or white paper towels dampened with water. It may be necessary to repeat the process several times for older or more stubborn stains.

MAYONNAISE (for removing white marks)
Apply a thin coat of mayonnaise over the white mark. Allow it to remain at least 1 hour. Then, wipe off with a clean soft cloth.

MERCUROCHROME
Mercurochrome can be used to repair scratches on some mahogany and cherry woods. Use a fine artist's brush to apply the mercurochrome being careful to keep it only on the scratch and not on the surrounding wood. Any stray liquid can be cleaned off with cotton swabs. Allow the mercurochrome to penetrate the scratch, then wipe off the excess with a clean cloth or white paper towels.

MILDEW (on wicker)
Rub the mildew spots with a cloth dipped in diluted household ammonia. Do not saturate the wicker. Rinse by wiping with a cloth dampened with water. Allow to air dry.

MILK STAINS (removing from a finish)
Milk stains, or stains caused by anything with a milk base (i.e.: ice cream, custard, etc.) need to be repaired as soon as possible for best results. Clean off any remaining foodstuff with a damp cloth. Apply paste silver polish to the spot with a soft damp cloth, or your finger. Gently rub the spot until the stain disappears. Wipe off any surface grit. Polish or wax furniture after repair.

MIRRORS ("patching" the silvering on the back of a mirror)

Carefully remove the wooden backing on the mirror. Measure the size of the damaged area on the silvered backing. Cut a piece of reflecting foil (or reflective film used for tinting windows) so that it is the size of the patch plus 1/2" on all sides. Carefully place over the damaged area. Use your fingers to smooth over the backing. Small pieces of scotch tape may be used to hold the patch in place. Replace the wooden backing.

METAL TRUNKS (cleaning)

Mix a mild solution of household cleaner and water. Apply with a sponge or a soft brush to clean off dirt and grime and loosen rust. Rinse the trunk by wiping with cloths moistened with water. Towel dry.

An alternative method: Mix 1/4 cup of dishwasher detergent into 1 gallon of very hot water. Apply with a sponge or soft cloth. Towel dry. No rinsing is required.

MOLD (removing)

To kill and remove mold, mix a solution of 1/2 cup of white vinegar and 1 gallon of room temperature water. Dip a soft cloth or sponge into the solution, then wring out until almost dry. Work on a small area at a time and gently rub the solution on the moldy area. Rinse by wiping with a clean cloth that has been dipped in clean water, and wrung out until almost dry. Blot the furniture dry when all mold has been removed.

MOTH BALLS
Place a few moth balls in your tool box with your metal tools to absorb moisture and prevent your tools from rusting.

NAIL POLISH (removing spilled nail polish)
Do not attempt to wipe up spilled nail polish until it has had a chance to dry! The solvents contained in most nail polishes will soften furniture finishes and you may end up wiping off the polish and the finish. Let the polish dry completely, then gently scrape it off with the edge of a plastic credit card. Do not use excessive pressure or you may bruise the wood.

NAIL POLISH (to prevent screwheads from rusting)
Loosen the screws so the heads are not in contact with the wood. Apply 1 or 2 coats of clear nail polish. (The clear coating will help prevent rust.) When the polish is dry, retighten the screws.

NAIL POLISH (to "touch-up" a clear finish)

Clear nail polish can often be used as a substitute for quick repairs on a varnish, shellac or lacquered finish. Lightly stroke the polish over the thin or chipped areas of the finish and then blend it with your finger to smooth it into the adjoining areas.

NAILS (removing stubborn)

If a stubborn nail keeps slipping through the claw of your claw hammer, and you can't attack it from a different angle without marring or denting the surrounding wood, clamp locking pliers over the nail shank, then slide the claw of the hammer under the jaws of the pliers. You will be able to remove the nail with ease.

NON-STICK COOKING SPRAY

Lightly spray your putty knife and other stripping tools with non-stick cooking spray to help keep the stripping gunk from adhering to them.

NUTMEATS (to repair scratches in the finish and the wood)

Rub freshly broken pieces of Brazil nuts, walnuts or pecans over the scratched area. The oil from the nut meat will penetrate the scratch and make it less noticeable.

NUTPICKS

Nutpicks make great stripping tools for getting into grooves in wood turnings and other hard to get to spots.

NYLON STOCKINGS AND PANTYHOSE (to apply finishes)

Wadded up nylon stockings and pantyhose (with the elastic waistband removed) can be used for applying stain or varnish when refinishing furniture. They are inexpensive, do not leave brush marks and can fit into areas that a brush can't.

NYLON STOCKINGS (to strain paint)

Pour paint through a nylon stocking into a paint bucket or paint tray. The stocking will act as an inexpensive, disposable filter.

ODORS IN WOODEN FURNITURE (removing)

Vacuum the furniture to remove any loose debris. Place the furniture outside, in the shade, on a nice warm sunny day if possible to allow it to "air out". After bringing in the furniture, put kitty litter, baking soda or other odor absorbent in the drawers, etc. Allow to remain for several days. Remove absorbent material and vacuum thoroughly. Wipe with a slightly dampened cloth to remove any remaining absorbent.

Cedar chips or cedar blocks can be placed in the cabinets and drawers to mask any remaining odors.

To seal the odors into the wood, brush a thinned coat of shellac or varnish on to the wood and allow to dry thoroughly.

ODORS ON UPHOLSTERED FURNITURE (removing)
Liberally sprinkle baking soda on the upholstery. Wait an hour or more, then vacuum.

OIL FINISH (repairing an oil finish)
Any type of finishing oil can be used to repair an oil finish. Moisten a soft cloth with water and wring out the excess moisture. Apply a small amount of oil to the dampened cloth. *Do not* apply the oil to the furniture. Lightly rub the wood, working on a small area at a time. Wait for several hours for the oil to be absorbed, then buff off the excess with a soft dry cloth.

Scratches and rings in an oil finish can usually be removed by gently rubbing the surface with fine steel wool lightly moistened with lemon oil or boiled linseed oil. Follow-up by buffing with a soft cloth. *Never* apply wax to furniture with an oil finish.

OLIVE OIL (to remove paper or labels stuck to the finish)

Never use a scraper or a metal knife to remove paper or labels stuck to the wood or the finish. Either one can damage the finish or bruise the wood. Instead, cover the area with a thin coating of olive oil or baby oil. Let the oil soak into the paper. Then rub the paper off with a soft cloth, or for stubborn spots use your fingernail or the edge of a plastic credit card.

ONIONS

Some stains can be removed from gilding by dabbing the surface gently with a raw onion.

OVEN CLEANER

Aerosol oven cleaner can be used to remove some stubborn paints and varnishes. Do not use on valuable pieces as the chemicals it contains may darken the wood. Neutralize the wood with white vinegar after stripping. Rinse with water and allow to dry before refinishing.

PAINT (removing fresh latex paint from a finish)

Dampen a soft cloth with water. Wring out the excess water, then wipe the finish until all of the paint is removed. It may necessary to re-wet the cloth and change the water frequently to avoid recontaminating the finish with softened paint. Turn and fold the cloth after every few wipes to avoid redistributing the paint. Difficult spots can be coaxed off by scraping with the edge of a plastic credit card in the direction of the grain. Follow-up by polishing or waxing the finish.

PAINT (removing fresh oil-based paint from a finish)

Wipe off oil-based paint immediately with a soft cloth or white paper towels dampened with turpentine. Wipe the finish until the paint is completely removed. Turn and fold the cloth if necessary to avoid recontamination or change cloths frequently.

An alternative method: Soften dry paint by wiping with a soft cloth moistened with linseed oil. Allow the linseed oil to penetrate, then wipe dry with another cloth. Difficult spots that do not wipe off can usually be removed by scraping with the edge of a plastic credit card in the direction of the wood grain.

PAINT (removing paint from metal outdoor furniture)

Spray the furniture with oven cleaner. Allow the cleaner to sit for about 15 minutes, then spray with a garden hose to remove.

PAINT (repairing a chipped finish)

Some paints can be "stretched". That is, the existing paint can be softened and then spread out over the chipped area. Paint stripper is used to soften oil-based paints. Water is used to soften latex paints. Use a small artist's brush. Moisten the brush in either water or paint stripper, depending on whether the paint is oil-based or latex. Lightly dab at the paint around the chipped area, the pull the softened paint over the chipped area. Continue softening and pulling until the chipped area is filled. It may be necessary to allow the paint to dry and repeat the technique several times to build-up enough coats to fill a dented chipped area.

PAINT BRUSHES (for dusting)

Use a natural bristle paint brushes to dust carved furniture and wicker or other woven furniture. The bristles can reach into small areas and crevices that a dust cloth can't.

PAINT BRUSHES (for stripping)

Trim the bristles on a paint brush so that you have a 1" long stump. These short bristles are great for getting old finish out of carving and grooves and other hard to reach places.

PAINT IN WOOD PORES (removing)

If paint remains in wood pores after stripping. Brush a coat of full strength shellac over the painted areas. Allow to dry. Then use remover to remove shellac and paint. The shellac will help pull the paint from the pores.

PAINT SPOTS (removing)

Latex paint spots can be removed by lightly wiping with a soft cloth or white paper towels that have been moistened with water. Follow by wiping the finish dry with a soft towel.

Oil-based paint spots can be removed by moistening a soft cloth with linseed oil and wiping over the paint spots. Allow the paint to penetrate, then wipe off with another clean soft cloth. Stubborn spots can be coaxed off with the edge of a plastic credit card. Do not use excessive pressure, and keep your strokes in the direction of the wood grain.

PANTY HOSE

Remove the elastic band from panty hose (or use old stockings) to polish your furniture. Wad them up in a ball, then buff the furniture. The nylon they contain acts as a mild abrasive and will polish without scratching. (Do not use on carved furniture or furniture with loose veneer as the nylon may snag on them.)

PASTE SHOE POLISH (to repair scratches)

Paste shoe polish will hide scratches quite well on some woods. Apply the polish to the scratch with a cotton swab. Allow to sit, then buff dry. If the polish is too dark, wipe it off with naptha, and try again with a lighter shade. Test the shoe polish in an inconspicuous area before making the repair. Shoe polish will develop a shine when buffed, and the resulting shiny area may not blend with the finish on the rest of the piece once the repair is done. The repair may become more noticeable than the scratch. Be careful to buff the polish only until the sheen matches the surrounding wood.

PEANUT BUTTER (to remove adhesive from finish)

Rub the adhesive area with smooth peanut butter. Allow to sit for a few minutes. Then wipe off with a soft cloth. Stubborn spots can be coaxed off with the edge of a plastic credit card.

PERFUME

Spray a small amount of perfume, or air freshener on your upholstered furniture to discourage cats from sharpening their claws on the furniture. Most cats will hate the smell and will avoid the furniture.

PET HAIR (removing)

Spray a small amount of hair spray on a facial tissue. While it is still tacky, lightly wipe over the upholstered furniture.

Or, put on a pair of rubber gloves and rub your hands over the furniture. The pet hair will become statically charged and stick to the rubber gloves.

PETROLEUM JELLY (to prevent rust on chrome)

Apply a thin coat of petroleum jelly to chrome pieces and lightly buff off before storing to prevent rust and pitting. Buff the remaining petroleum jelly off before reusing the piece of furniture.

PETROLEUM JELLY (to remove white marks)

A liberal coat of petroleum jelly can be an effective, non-abrasive method of white spot removal for some finishes. Spread the petroleum jelly over the damaged area. Allow it to remain for 24 to 48 hours. Then wipe off the excess. Petroleum jelly is a great spot removal method for large areas.

PIANO (cleaning)

To safely remove fingerprints from a piano with a high glass shine, wipe with a dampened chamois then dry with another dry chamois.

PIANO KEYS (cleaning)
Ivory piano keys can be cleaned by lightly rubbing with a Pink Pearl Eraser .

PIANO KEYS (cleaning)
Combine 1/4 cup of water and 3 tablespoons of rubbing alcohol. Apply a small amount of the solution to a soft cloth and lightly wipe the keys, taking care not to get any excess solution between the keys or on the piano itself.

PIANO KEYS (whitening)
Piano keys can be whitened by rubbing them with a soft cloth dipped into 2 parts salt and 1 part lemon juice. Or baking soda and a small amount of water. Or regular (not gel) toothpaste. Be very careful not to get the paste in the crevices between the keys. Wipe the paste off with a damp cloth. Then buff with a dry cloth until completely dry.

Note: Ivory will turn yellow if it is continuously kept from light. Keep the piano top closed, but keep the keyboard exposed.

PICKLE JUICE
Pickle juice (or a solution of white vinegar and salt) can be used to age brass hardware and give it a verdigris finish. Clean the hardware and lightly abrade it with a piece of fine steel wool. Dip the hardware in the pickle juice or vinegar solution (or brush it on for larger pieces) and then allow to sit for

about an hour. Repeat the process until you achieve the desired color. The hardware should be coated with spray lacquer once dry to preserve the new "old" look.

PIE TINS
Place a pie tin under the legs of furniture before stripping. When the stripper runs down off the leg and into the container you can recycle it and use it again.

PIE TINS
Use tin snips to cut aluminum pie pans in half. Then use the aluminum half circles as disposable scrapers when stripping paint or thick finishes.

PLASTIC TABLE TOPS
Plastic table tops can be cleaned and shined by rubbing a small dab of regular (not gel) toothpaste onto the table top with a soft cloth dampened with water. Wipe clean with another cloth dampened with clean water and dry thoroughly to prevent water spots.

PLASTIC WRAP (prolonging the shelf life of paint or varnish)
Apply a piece of plastic wrap on top of the paint or varnish in the can before closing to prevent a skin from forming and

to prevent foreign objects and dried finish or paint from falling into the can when it is reopened.

PLASTIC WRAP
(See : SCREWS, easier insertion)

PLEXIGLASS CLEANER
Mix one quart of water and 1 capful of liquid fabric softener together to make a great lint-free cleaner. Apply to the plexiglass surface with a clean cloth. Buff dry with another clean cloth. Change cloths frequently.

PUTTY KNIVES
Use a file to round off the corners of a putty knife before using on furniture. The sharp corners can gouge and scratch the wood.

"Q-TIPS"

Wrap a small piece of steel wool around the end of a Q-tip and use to remove stripper, wax, etc. from carvings and fluted areas.

QUIETING A SQUEAKY BED FRAME

If a wooden bed frame makes a squeaky noise when weight is put on the mattress, it is probably caused by the wood surfaces of the frame rubbing together. To correct this problem, remove the mattress and box springs. Melt a small amount of paraffin over a double-boiler. Then pour the melted paraffin into all of the joints and corners of the bed frame. Allow it to cool completely. When the paraffin hardens, it will act as a lubricant between the wood surfaces and will silence the squeak. Melt more paraffin and reapply if necessary.

RADIATOR CLAMPS/HOSE CLAMPS

Use radiator clamps or hose clamps to clamp or hold round pieces of wood together during repairs. The round shape will apply even pressure all the way around and the screw will allow the clamp to be tightened to just the right amount of pressure.

ROCKING CHAIR ROCKERS (preventing them from marking the finish on, or wearing the finish off a floor)

Place strips of adhesive tape along the length of the underside of each rocker.

An alternative method: Wax the bottoms of the rockers.

ROLLTOP DESK (lubricating a stubborn top)

Use a white candle, a small piece of paraffin or a small bar of soap and rub inside the groove that contains the rolltop on both sides of the desk. Roll the top up and down the groove several times to coat the ends of the slats on the rolltop. Peri-

odic applications of paraffin or soap will keep the rolltop working smoothly.

RUBBER BALLS

Split a rubber ball in half. Place a steel wool pad inside the
ball half to protect your hands from steel wool splinters and
to make the pad easier to grip when rubbing out stain or a
finish coat.

RUBBER BANDS

Stretch a wide rubber band vertically around an open container of paint, stain or varnish. Use the rubber band to wipe
the excess from the brush each time it is dipped into the can
instead of wiping on the rim. This will prevent build-up in
the rim and will prevent the lid from sticking when it is re-
sealed.

RUBBER BANDS (monitoring repair supplies)

A good way to monitor liquid repair supplies in opaque bottles
(i.e.: glue, paint, etc.) at a glance is to wrap a rubber band
around each container at the level of the contents. Move the
rubber band after each use.

RUBBER BANDS (repairing casters)

A temporary caster repair for loose casters that keep falling out of their sockets can be made by wrapping a rubber band around the shaft of the caster, then re-insert it into the socket.

RUBBER CEMENT (for removing stains from leather)
Apply a thick layer of rubber cement over the stained area. Peel off the cement when it is almost completely dry. The cement will lift off the stain.

RUSH (repairing a sagging seat)
Older rush seats have a tendency to sag because the rushes dry out and break down. If the rushes are simply dry and not badly broken, the sag may perk up by lightly spraying the seat with water, then leaving it to dry away from direct sunlight, but in an area with good circulation. The procedure can be repeated several times.

RUST SPOTS (removing from chrome)
Rub the rust spots with a crumpled up piece of aluminum foil dipped in cola. Rinse with water and dry.

RUSTY NUTS, BOLTS AND SCREWS (loosening)
Pour club soda (or just about any other carbonated beverage) over the rusty areas or cover the rusty areas with a cloth or a piece of paper towel soaked in soda. The carbonated bubbles help to loosen and remove rust.

An alternative method: Apply a drop or two of ammonia to the rusted area.

SALAD OIL (for removing adhesive from a finish)

Apply salad oil to a soft cloth (or your finger) and rub on the adhesive spot. Allow to sit for a few minutes, then wipe off with a clean soft cloth. Any stubborn spots that remain can be lightly scraped off with the edge of a plastic credit card. Be sure not to use excessive pressure and always follow the grain of the wood.

SALIVA

You can clean small dirty areas on furniture and nooks and crevices that are hard to reach by other methods by licking a Q-Tip swab and then using it to lightly rub the area. Saliva contains enzymes that dissolve accumulated dirt and grime. It registers around 7.5 on a pH scale so it is less alkaline than baking soda (which registers 8.4) or ammonia (which registers at 11.9) and is less acidic than vinegar. It is harmless to even the most delicate finish ... and it works!

SALT (to remove grease stains from upholstery)
Sprinkle the grease stain with salt. Lightly brush it into the stain and let it sit until the stain is absorbed. Brush off any excess with a slightly dampened cloth.

SALT (to remove stains from wicker)
Moisten your finger or a soft cloth with water then dip into salt and lightly rub over wicker to help remove stubborn stains. Rinse with clear water and allow to dry thoroughly

SANDPAPER
Reinforce the back of a piece of sandpaper with strips of masking tape to make it last longer.

SANDPAPER
Sandpaper will resist cracking and last longer if the backing is slightly dampened before use. Wrap the paper around a sanding block or a piece of wood to make the sanding more efficient.

SAWDUST
Pour some woodworker's glue or white glue on to a piece of waxed paper. Mix in sawdust a little at a time until it forms a pasty dough consistency. Use the paste to fill cracks and dents in wood.

SAWDUST

Apply a light coat of sawdust over the top of a coat of furniture stripper, then wipe with paper towels or rags. The sawdust will help absorb the moisture from the stripper and make removal easier.

SCRATCHES (removing from a lacquer finish)

Scratches in a lacquer finish can be repaired by dipping a very fine brush into lacquer thinner, and then lightly stroking over the scratch with the moistened bristles. Continue to brush over the scratch until the finish surrounding the scratch softens and fills in the scratch.

SCRATCHES (removing from a shellac finish)

Scratches in a shellac finish can be repaired by dipping a very fine brush into denatured alcohol, and then lightly stroking over the scratch with the moistened bristles. Continue to brush over the scratch until the finish surrounding the scratch softens and fills in the scratch.

SCRATCHES (removing from a varnish finish)

Minor scratches in a varnish finish can often be removed by lightly rubbing the scratches with a soft, lint-free cloth moistened with turpentine.

SCRATCHES (removing from brown mahogany)

Old iodine turns brown with age, and works very well for repairing scratches in brown mahogany. Use a fine artist's brush to apply the iodine to the scratch. Be careful to keep the iodine on the scratch and off of the surrounding wood finish. Allow the iodine to penetrate, then wipe off any excess with a clean rag or white paper towels.

SCRATCHES (removing from dark wood)

Mix 1 teaspoon of instant coffee and 2 teaspoons of water. Apply to the scratch with a cotton swab or small artist's brush.

SCRATCHES (removing from maple)

Scratches in maple wood can be repaired by mixing a solution of 50% iodine and 50% denatured alcohol. Use a fine artist's brush to apply the mixture to the scratch. Be careful to keep the mixture on the scratch and off of the surrounding wood finish. Allow the solution to penetrate the scratch, then wipe off any excess with a clean cloth or white paper towels.

SCRATCHES (removing from red mahogany)

Scratches in red mahogany can be repaired by brushing with iodine. Carefully apply the iodine to the scratch with a very fine brush. Take care to keep the iodine on the scratch and off of the surrounding wood finish. Allow the iodine to penetrate, then wipe off any excess with a clean cloth or white paper towels.

SCRATCHES (removing from teak wood)

Minor scratches in teak wood can often be repaired by brushing with a solution of 50% linseed oil and 50% turpentine. Use a very fine brush to apply the solution. Allow it to penetrate the scratch, then wipe off the excess with a soft cloth or white paper towels.

SCRATCHES (removing from wood furniture)

Apply a small dab of conditioning hairdressing (like Alberto VO5 Conditioning Hairdressing) on a clean soft cloth. Rub over the scratch in the wood. Then buff with a dry soft cloth.

SCREWDRIVERS

Rub the blade of a screwdriver with chalk before use to keep it from slipping out of the screwheads.

SCREWS (a general tip)

Screws can only enter the wood at the rate their threads cut the wood. Applying more pressure to a hard-to-turn screw is *not* the answer. Use a large-handled screwdriver with a blade as wide as the screw's slot.

SCREWS (a general tip)

To help you remember which way to turn the screw just remember: "left is loose and right is tight".

SCREWS (easier insertion)

Rub the threads of screws with soap before inserting and they will drive into wood much easier.

An alternative method: Push the screw through a small piece of plastic wrap. Put the screwdriver into the groove in the head of the screw then pull the plastic wrap up and over the head of the screw and the blade of the screwdriver. Then screw the screw into the wood.

SCREWS (tightening loose)

This works well for screws that are slightly loose in their sockets. Remove the screw. Paint the threads with nail polish. Then reinsert the screw. The screw will be tighter when the polish dries.

An alternative method: remove a few strands of steel wool from a steel wool pad. Wrap the steel wool around the screw threads, then insert the screw.

Another alternative method: Place toothpicks in the hole, then replace the screw as usual.

SCUFF MARKS (removing)

Dip a small piece of 3/0 or 4/0 steel wool into turpentine or mineral spirits. Lightly rub the scuff marks in the finish. When the marks are removed, wipe off any excess turpentine or mineral spirits with white paper towels or a clean cloth. Apply a coat of wax or furniture polish to the area to help prevent future scuff marks

SHAVING CREAM

Apply shaving cream sparingly to upholstery stain. Then rub gently with a damp cloth. Allow to air dry.

SHELLAC FINISH (reviving)

A shellac finish can be revived and made to look "new" again without refinishing. Mix together a solution of 2 parts mineral oil (or olive oil) and 1 part clear shellac. Apply the oil mixture to a soft cloth and lightly rub the shellac surface, making sure to keep your strokes with the grain.

SHOE POLISH

Cream shoe polish can be used to touch-up scratches in the finish or lighter stained areas in the wood. Apply a small amount of shoe polish to a soft cloth. Rub over the area to be repaired, then lightly buff with a soft cloth. Be sure not to buff too much if the repair is on a flat finish. Buffing will increase the shine of the polish.

SILICONES (removing)

The best way to remove silicones is with turpentine. Moisten a clean cloth or white paper towels with turpentine, and rub a small area of the contaminated surface. Dry thoroughly with a clean cloth or clean paper towels. Continue in this manner, changing cloths or towels when necessary, until the whole piece of furniture has been done. Then, using clean cloths, repeat the procedure to make sure the surface is no longer contaminated with silicones. Decontamination is especially important if you are preparing to apply a new finish or repair an existing finish, as no finish can be successfully applied over a silicone contaminated surface.

SILLY PUTTY
Use a small piece of Silly Putty to clean lint, dirt and "what-have-you" out of the crevices on upholstered furniture.

SILVER POLISH (to remove white water marks from a finish)
Moisten your finger or a soft cloth, then apply a small amount of silver polish. Lightly rub the polish on the white mark until it is removed. Do not use excessive pressure, and stop frequently to check on your progress. Wipe off any excess polish once the white mark is removed. Apply a coat of wax or polish to the area, if necessary, to cover any dullness in the finish that may occur.

SLATE (cleaning)
Slate tabletops are very porous and absorbent so care must be taken to avoid over-wetting the slate. Mix together 1-1/2 tablespoons of washing soda and 1 gallon of warm water. Stir to mix. Use a sponge slightly dampened in the solution to clean the slate surface. Take care not to wet the surrounding wood. Rinse with clear water and blot dry.

Do not use soap solutions on slate surfaces.

SLATE (polishing)

Slate can be given a buffed and polished look by rubbing with a soft cloth dampened with linseed oil. Rub into the surface, then buff off the excess.

SOCKS

Put a sock on your hand and run your hand over a sanded wood surface to test for rough spots. Re-sand where the sock hits a snag.

SOY SAUCE

Soy sauce can be used to cover scratches in wood. Lightly brush on the scratch with a cotton swab. The soy sauce may need to be diluted with water to achieve the proper wood tone to match the surrounding wood.

SPATULAS

An old cooking spatula makes a great stripping tool for flat surfaces. Hold the spatula upside down and push it to remove softened gunk.

Plastic spatulas can also be used to protect furniture surfaces when removing nails. Place the blade of the spatula under the head of a hammer while you are levering out the nail.

SPLINTERS (removing from your finger)

If you get a splinter in your finger from working on a wooden project, it can often be removed by covering the splinter with a small piece of packing tape, lightly applying pressure to the tape, then gently removing it.

Another method to make removing splinters easier: Soak the area surrounding the splinter with olive oil. Then use tweezers or a needle to remove the splinter.

If you are having trouble locating the splinter, use a swab dipped in iodine to coat the general area where you suspect the splinter to be. Iodine will make the splinter more visible.

SPLINTERS IN WOOD (repairing)

Use a toothpick or a sewing needle to carefully remove any dirt, dust or threads from the splinter. Be careful not to lift or bend the wood. Inject a few drops of glue behind the splinter or apply the glue with a toothpick. Push the splinter back into place and wipe off any excess glue that squeezes out. Apply pressure on the splinter with your thumb and secure the splinter in place with a piece of masking tape. Allow the glue to dry for approximately 12 hours, then carefully remove the tape.

SPRAY PAINT (touch-up tip)

To prevent spray paint from "globbing" on the surface when you are trying to touch-up a small area. Cut a hole the size of the area to be sprayed in the center of a folded newspaper.

Then, center the hole over the spot and peak the fold slightly above the surface. Spray the paint, making several passes across the hole. The raised paper will allow some of the residual spray to go beneath the paper creating feathered edges instead of "globs".

SPRAY PAINT (without the messy over-spray)
Place the furniture item that you are going to paint inside an old large appliance box with the front cut off to create a mini-spray booth.

SQUEAKY BED SPRINGS
Use a tack remover or flat blade screwdriver to remove the fabric covering the bottom of the box spring mattress. Spray the springs with a graphite lubricant or WD-40. Use a staple gun to fasten the fabric back in place.

STEEL WOOL
Do not use steel wool to rub out the wood before or between coats of any water-based products. Small strands of the steel wool may get caught in the wood and can cause rust spots.

STICKING DRAWERS
Remove the drawer. Rub a white candle or paraffin on the drawer track. Replace drawer.

SUEDE
Suede can not be cleaned like regular leather and most dirt or stains should be removed by a professional. Minor stains can often be removed by lightly rubbing the stain with an art gum eraser, then lightly brushing with a suede brush.

SUGAR
Sprinkle sugar on your hands before lathering up with soap and water if you are trying to remove a lot of dirt and grime. Your hands will get cleaner quicker.

SUNTAN LOTION (removing paint from hands)
Squeeze a small amount of suntan lotion onto painty hands and rub together. Wipe clean with paper towels. (Suntan lotion works very effectively and is more gentle to your hands than paint thinner or turpentine.)

See also: FORMICA FURNITURE TOPS, (cleaning)
See also: VINYL FURNITURE, (removing ink stains)

TABLE LEAVES

A tip to prevent a repair: Put the table leaves in the table occasionally so they are exposed to the same light and humidity as the table. This will help to maintain the same color on the table and the leaves. The table should also be turned several times during the year, if possible, to maintain a more even color.

TABLES (lubricating a wooden extension mechanism)

Extend the table top as wide as possible to expose the entire length of the wood runners. Use a sharp knife or chisel blade to scrape the accumulated dirt, wax, or lubricant from the runners. Be careful not to gouge the wood. Use turpentine or mineral spirits on a soft cloth if necessary to remove wax or grease, then wipe with a clean, dry cloth. Rub a piece of paraffin or a white candle in the runners to coat them with a thin coat of wax. Open and close the table a few times to help evenly distribute the new lubricant.

TEA

Mix together 1 cup of cooled black leaf tea and 1/4 cup of vinegar. Moisten a soft cloth with the solution. Wring out any excess, then wash accumulated dirt and grime from wooden furniture. Rinse if you prefer. Dry by buffing with clean cloths or towels.

See also: BLACK LACQUER FURNITURE, (cleaning)

TEAK WOOD (repairing scratches)

Small scratches in teak wood can be repaired by rubbing with a solution of 50% linseed oil and 50% turpentine. Buff after application to remove any excess.

Small cracks in outdoor teak wood furniture are the result of natural expansion and contraction of the wood. They are harmless and generally need no repair. Minor scratches can be repaired by lightly buffing with fine sandpaper.

TENNIS BALLS

Cut a hole in a tennis ball. Place the ball over the head of a regular hammer to create a safe mallet for furniture repairs.

TEST TO DETERMINE THE FINISH

Find an inconspicuous place on the furniture and clean off all accumulated polish, wax or dirt. Moisten a cotton swab with denatured alcohol and rub the cleaned area. Rub for a few minutes, remoistening the swab if necessary. If the finish is shellac the denatured alcohol will soften it and begin to remove the finish. If the finish does not soften apply lacquer thinner to a cotton swab and rub the cleaned area. Rub for a few minutes, remoistening the swab if necessary. If the finish is lacquer, lacquer thinner will soften it and begin to remove the finish. A varnish finish will not be affected by either denatured alcohol or lacquer thinner.

TEST TO DETERMINE WHETHER TO USE PAINT REMOVER OR FURNITURE REFINISHER

Moisten a cotton ball with a small amount of nail polish remover and touch it to the furniture in an inconspicuous place. If the cotton ball sticks, use refinisher to strip the furniture. If the cotton ball doesn't stick use paint remover to strip the furniture.

THREAD SPOOLS

Empty, wooden thread spools can be made into clamps to help apply pressure during repairs which require gluing. You will need 2 wooden spools, a bolt narrow enough to fit through the spool holes and long enough to fit through both spools and the thickness of the wood to be glued, and a wing nut. Insert the bolt through the spools. Place the workpiece between the "jaws" of the 2 spools, then tighten the wing nut to close the jaws.

TIN (removing rust)
Dip a 4/0 steel wool pad in mineral oil or vegetable oil and lightly rub the rusted areas. Buff off remaining oil with a soft cloth.

TOOLS (preventing rust)
Keep a few pieces of chalk in your toolbox to absorb moisture and prevent tools from rusting.

Cut an old garden hose into pieces, and then slit the pieces lengthwise. Place over the edges of sawblades to protect the teeth and prevent rust.

TOOTHBRUSHES
Dip a toothbrush into furniture polish and use to apply the polish to hard to reach areas like carvings and decorative trim. Blot with a soft cloth and buff to remove excess polish.

TOOTHPASTE (to remove fine scratches from mirrors)
Apply a small dab of tooth-whitening toothpaste (not the gel kind) to your finger or a soft cloth. Lightly rub it on the mirror surface in a circular motion. When scratches are removed, remove excess toothpaste with a soft cloth dampened with water, then dry thoroughly.

TOOTHPASTE (to remove white water marks from a finish)

Slightly dampen your finger or a soft cloth. Apply a small amount of toothpaste (not the gel kind). Lightly rub the toothpaste on the white mark. Rub with the grain of the wood. When the mark is removed, wipe off the excess toothpaste with a soft cloth slightly dampened with water. Dry thoroughly.

TRUNKS (removing odors)

Soak a slice of bread in white vinegar. Put the bread on a plate and place in the trunk. Close the trunk lid and allow the bread to remain for at least 12 hours.

TURPENTINE (to remove silicone furniture polish)

Moisten a clean soft cloth or white paper towels with turpentine, and rub a small area of the surface. Dry thoroughly with a clean cloth. Continue in this manner, changing towels or cloths when necessary, until the whole piece of furniture has been done. Then, using clean cloths, repeat the procedure to make sure the surface is no longer contaminated. Decontamination is especially important if you are preparing to apply a new finish or repair an existing finish, as no finish can be successfully applied over a silicone contaminated surface.

TURPENTINE (to remove "stickies and gummies" from furniture)

Moisten a clean soft cloth or white paper towels with turpentine. Lightly rub the gummy sticky area. Follow up by wiping with a clean soft cloth.

If the build-up is really thick, moisten a small piece of cloth with turpentine and lay it over the area. Allow it to cover the area for about 20 minutes. Remove the cloth and wipe with a clean dry cloth.

TWINE

Use coarse twine to remove stripping sludge from fine turnings and grooves. Hold one end in each hand and rub back and forth as you would a shoe shine rag.

UPHOLSTERY CLEANER ("do-it-yourself")
Formula #1

Mix 1/2 cup of mild detergent with 2 cups of boiling water. Cool until it forms a jelly consistency. Use an electric hand mixer to beat it into a stiff foam. Use as you would commercial upholstery cleaner.

UPHOLSTERY CLEANER ("do-it-yourself")
Formula #2
Mix 1/4 cup of vegetable-oil-based liquid soap (like Murphy Oil Soap) with 3 tablespoons of water. Whip with a wire whip until a thick foam forms on the top. Remove the foam and use as you would a commercial upholstery cleaner. Continue to whip the mixture in the bowl and remove foam as needed.

UPHOLSTERY FABRIC (removing impressions)
To raise the nap back to normal and remove the impression, lay a piece of woolen fabric over the spot. On top of that place a piece of dampened muslin. Heat an electric clothes iron to the "cotton/linen" setting and rub the iron back and forth over the muslin. The wool will protect the napped fabric, while the steam from the muslin passes through to soften the crushed nap. Remove the cloths and carefully brush up the nap with a toothbrush. Allow the fabric to dry thoroughly before use. The process may have to be repeated for stubborn impressions.

UPHOLSTERY FABRIC (cleaning)
See also ERASERS

UPHOLSTERY FABRICS (removing excessive lint)
Dark upholstery fabrics that collect excessive lint can be cleaned by rubbing with old nylon stockings or pantyhose.

UPHOLSTERY FABRIC (removing stains)
See also: CHOCOLATE (removing stains from upholstery
See also: CLUB SODA (removing stains from upholstery)

UPHOLSTERY TACKS
Use a wooden thread spool when hammering decorative up-holstery tacks to avoid damaging the head of the tack. Place the hole in the spool against the head of the tack, then hit the spool with the hammer.

UPHOLSTERY TACKS
Stick a few extra decorative tacks to a hidden spot on the furniture so they will be available for replacements if necessary.

VARNISH (removing from your hands)
Spray your hands with Spray 'N Wash laundry stain remover, rub them together, then wash with soap and water.

VERDIGRIS (removing from brass)

Verdigris, the greenish coating that appears on brass and some other metal surfaces, can be removed by scrubbing with a mixture of ammonia and water. Rinse with clear water, then dry thoroughly to avoid water spots.

VERDIGRIS (repairing)

A damaged verdigris finish can be repaired by using "Patina Green" or a similar brass "aging" product. Use a fine artist brush to brush the solution over the scratch until a dull film appears. Allow the solution to air dry. Additional coats may be needed to achieve the desired color. Allow each coat to dry completely before applying the next one. Apply a coat of lacquer over the repaired area for protection when the repair is complete, if desired.

VINEGAR (to reduce static on vinyl seats)

Clean the seats thoroughly, then add white vinegar to the rinse water to reduce static from forming. Dry with soft towels to prevent water spots.

VINEGAR (to remove glue)

Use undiluted white vinegar to remove glue from a furniture finish by moistening a soft cloth then lightly rubbing the glue. When the glue is gone, wipe with a soft cloth slightly dampened with water, then buff dry with a soft cloth.

Undiluted white vinegar can also be used to dissolve glue

when removing a caned seat. Use an eyedropper to saturate the spline and soften the glue that holds it in the groove.

VINEGAR (to remove rust)
Soak rusty tools or screws and bolts in undiluted white vinegar. Allow to soak overnight for severe cases of rust. Rinse off the vinegar then buff dry.

VINYL FURNITURE (cleaning)
Dissolve 1/4 cup dishwasher detergent in one gallon of very hot water. Dip a sponge or soft brush into the solution and scrub the grease and grime from the furniture. Wipe clean with a dry towel. Most dishwasher detergents contain water-softening agents so that the vinyl will be shiny clean and spot-free without rinsing.

(See also: CHALK (to clean vinyl)

VINYL FURNITURE (removing ink stains)
Apply a small amount of vegetable shortening to the ink stain with a soft cloth. Lightly rub until the stain is removed. Buff to remove any excess shortening.

An alternative method: Apply a small amount of suntan lotion to a soft cloth. Lightly rub the area until the stain is removed. Buff to remove any excess.

VODKA (as a metal polish)

Mix 3 tablespoons of vodka, 1/2 cup diatomaceaous earth and 1/2 teaspoon vegetable-oil-based liquid soap (like Murphy Oil Soap) together in a jar. Add enough water to the mixture to make a thick paste. You can use this solution as a general metal polish. Use as you would commercial polish: Apply with a soft dampened cloth or sponge. Rub the tarnished metal until clean. Rinse and then dry thoroughly.

VODKA (to remove hairspray or lacquer over-spray from mirrors)

Mix 4 teaspoons of vodka and 1 pint of water in a spray bottle. Mix thoroughly. Spray the solution on a soft cloth and rub the mirror surface to clean. Do not spray the solution directly on the mirror as it may leak onto the back and damage the silvering. Buff the mirror dry with a clean soft cloth.

WARPAGE (removing from a table leaf or flat table top)

Remove the table top from the base. Place the table top or leaf, concave side down, on a wet grassy yard in the sun. The dry side of the board (the concave side) will absorb moisture from the grass and the convex side will dry out by the heat of the sun.

WARPAGE (removing from wooden trunk and chest tops)
Place a large plastic container of water inside the empty trunk or chest then close the lid. Allow the water to remain inside for several weeks. The water will increase the humidity on the inside of the trunk or chest, and will help to re-swell the wood fibers and straighten the warp. It will also help close small cracks in the wood.

WAX (removing spilled candle wax)
Candle wax should be removed from a finish as soon as possible after the wax has had a chance to cool. Do not use a knife or other metal object to scrape the wax as they may damage the finish or dent the wood. Instead, wrap several ice cubes in a piece of plastic wrap or put them in a sandwich baggie, and then place on the wax. Allow the wax to harden. Then use the edge of a plastic credit card to gently push the wax off of the surface. In most cases the wax will come off all at once in one piece. If it doesn't, replace the ice pack and repeat the process. Any waxy residue can be removed by rubbing the area briskly with a soft cloth. The heat and friction generated by the rubbing will remove any trace of remaining wax.

WAXPAPER (to protect wood while gluing)

Place small pieces of wax paper between the wood and the clamps (especially wooden clamps) when gluing to prevent clamps from sticking to the wood.

WAXPAPER (to retard stripper)

Help slow down the evaporation of furniture strippers and concentrate their strength by covering wet stripper with a piece of wax paper.

"WEATHERING" WOODEN OUTDOOR FURNITURE

Mix 1-1/2 to 2 cups of baking soda into 1 gallon of water. Scrub the mixture into the wood surface. Then rinse off with clear water.

WHISKEY

Mix together 1/8 cup of whiskey, 1/4 cup of linseed oil and 1/8 cup of lemon juice in a small jar. Shake until thoroughly blended. Soak a soft, lint-free cloth in the solution, then wring out. Shake the cloth to remove any excess. Use the cloth to polish wood furniture. Buff with a clean cloth after application.

WICKER FURNITURE (lighten unpainted)

Wash wicker with a mild solution of laundry bleach and water. Rinse with clean water then allow to dry out of direct sunlight. The wicker must be completely dry to get an accurate idea of the bleached color, as damp wicker will appear darker than it really is. Old wicker tends to be more porous than new wicker, so do a spot test with the solution on a small spot on the underside of the furniture first to see how it will affect that particular piece of wicker.

WICKER (preventing splitting and drying out)

Painted wicker and unpainted wicker should both be wetted down on a regular basis to keep the wicker fibers from splitting and drying out. This is also a great way to clean off dust and dirt that has settled into the weave. Small pieces of wicker can be sprayed with a spray bottle or put in the shower. Larger pieces can be taken outside and sprayed with the garden hose. Do not use excessive water pressure. Once the piece is thoroughly wet, allow it to dry out of direct sunlight and away from any direct source of heat.

WICKER FURNITURE (removing creaking noises)

Wicker furniture creaks because it is dry. Wetting down the wicker will add moisture to the fibers and prevent or eliminate the creaking sound. Small pieces of wicker can be sprayed with a spray bottle or placed in the shower and wetted down. Larger pieces can be taken outside and sprayed with a garden hose. After the piece is thoroughly wet, allow it to dry out of direct sunlight and away from any source of direct heat.

WICKER FURNITURE (removing stubborn stains)

Dip a moistened finger or soft cloth into some table salt. Rub over the stained area. Rinse with clear water, then allow the wicker to air dry.

WICKER FURNITURE (removing "wicker whiskers")

Wicker tends to develop "whiskers" – fuzzy fibers that become roughed up from wear. The roughness can be removed by lightly rubbing the whiskers with very fine (3/0) sandpaper. Use very light pressure, and be careful to sand with the grain of the wicker.

WOOD DISINFECTANT

Mix together 1 teaspoon of borax powder, 1/4 teaspoon of vegetable-oil-based liquid soap (like Murphy Oil Soap) and 1 cup of hot water. Put the solution in an empty spray bottle. Spray on the wood, scrub with a sponge if desired and then rinse by wiping with a clean damp cloth. Buff dry.

WOODEN CHAIRS (eliminating squeaks)

Wooden chairs generally start to squeak because of moisture loss in the wood. As the wood dries, the dowels shrink, and no longer fit properly in their cavities resulting in movement and noise. Water can be applied to the dowel cavities to swell the wood fibers. Use an eye dropper to apply water to the joints then wipe off any excess to prevent damage to the finish. Or apply a wood expanding fluid (like Chair-Loc) to the cavities and then wipe off the excess to prevent staining. The wood expanding fluid will penetrate the wood and permanently expand the wood fibers.

WOODEN FURNITURE WITH A POLYURETHANE FINISH (cleaning)

Dissolve 1/4 cup dishwasher detergent into 1 gallon of very hot water. Scrub the dirt, grease and grime from the furniture with a sponge or soft cloth. Wipe clean with a dry towel. Most dishwasher detergents contain water-softening agents and will leave the surface clean and shiny without rinsing.

WORCESTERSHIRE SAUCE (to clean brass)

Pour a generous amount of Worcestershire sauce on a clean sponge or soft cloth. Rub onto the brass pieces and allow to remain for at least 1 hour. Badly tarnished pieces will need additional time. Really badly tarnished items may need to soak overnight. Rinse with hot water. Dry thoroughly.

WORCESTERSHIRE SAUCE (to cover scratches in wood)

Use a cotton swab or small artist's brush to apply Worcestershire sauce to the scratch in the wood. The Worcestershire sauce may need to be diluted with water to achieve the proper wood tone to match the surrounding wood.

"X" JOINTS (CROSS JOINTS - clamping and gluing loose)

The most effective way to clamp the cross joints on a table or chair without expensive clamps is to use elastic tie-down cords or a piece of clothesline. The tie-down cords can be interconnected to achieve the proper length to go around the joint area. A piece of clothesline can be tied around the joints and then tightened like a tourniquet. Do not over-tighten the joints or apply excessive pressure. Use woodworker's glue or white glue when gluing wooden furniture. Wipe off any excess glue with a dampened cloth or paper towel.

YARN (to tighten loose casters or loose screws)

Wrap a small piece of thin yarn around the stem of a loose

caster before inserting it back into the hole to help prevent it from falling out again.

Wrap a small piece of thin yarn around a screw before inserting it back into its hole. The yarn will make the screw fit tighter.

YOGURT (to "age" outdoor cement benches, etc.)
Scoop the yogurt out of the container with your hands and apply a thick coating of plain yogurt to the cement. Allow to sit for several hours, or overnight if possible. Use a garden hose to rinse off any remaining yogurt. The yogurt will "age" the furniture and give it a slightly marbled, patinaed finish. The process may be repeated if you would like to increase the affect.

ZIPPERS (on upholstered furniture)
Furniture may have zippers on the pillows, cushions, etc. but this does not necessarily mean the covers are removable or washable. The zippers are used during the manufacturing process to ensure an even fit of the material, and to aid in the construction of the furniture.

Zippers on covers that are removable and washable can become stubborn after washing, or just from age or use. To make the zipper glide easier rub a lead pencil back and forth a few times over the zipper teeth. Or rub a bar of soap on the teeth. Then open and close the zipper a few times to evenly distribute the lubricant on the zipper.

Trademark Information

"Alberto VO5 Conditioning Hairdressing" is a registered trademark of Alberto-Culver USA Inc.

"ARMOR ALL Vinyl Protectant" is a registered trademark of Armor All Products Corp., Irvine, CA.

"Chair-Loc" is a registered trademark of The Chair-Loc Company, Lakehurst, New Jersey.

"Formica" brand laminate is a registered trademark of Formica Corporation, Cincinnati, Ohio

"Jell-O" is a registered trademark of Kraft Foods, Inc.

"Murphy Oil Soap" is a registered trademark of Colgate-Palmolive Company, New York, New York.

"Patina Green" is a registered trademark of Modern Options, Inc., San Fransisco, CA.

"Pink Pearl Eraser" is a registered trademark of Sanford.

"Q-Tip Swabs" is a registered trademark of Johnson & Johnson, Inc., Skillman , New Jersey

"Silly Putty" is a registered trademark of Binney & Smith, Easton, PA

"Spray ' n Wash" is a registered trademark of Dow Brands L. P..

"TSP" is a registered trademark of America's Finest Products, Corp., Santa Monica, CA

"WD-40" is a registered trademark of WD-40 Company, San Diego, CA.

"Worcestershire Sauce" is a registered trademark of Lea & Perrins, Inc., Fair Lawn, New Jersey.

Index

to lubricate a stubborn rolltop desk top, 64-65
to repair sticking drawers, 77

Cane,
repairing a sagging seat, 19

Canvas seats,
cleaning, 20

Car wax,
to protect aluminum furniture, 11
to rejuvenate a dull finish on Formica brand laminate surfaces, 32
to rejuvenate a dull finish on plastic furniture, 32

Carbonated beverages,
to loosen rusty nuts, bolts and screws, 66

Cardboard box,
spray painting tip, 77

Carrying marble furniture,
tip to prevent damage, 47

Carved furniture,
dusting, 56
stripping tip, 57, 63

Casters,
repairing loose, 20, 95-96
repairing, 65

Castor oil,
for reviving leather, 20

Catsup,
for cleaning brass, 21

Cedar chests,
restoring the smell, 21

Cedar chips,
to remove odors from wooden furniture, 53

Cement,
"aging" cement benches, 96

Chalk,
for repairing marble, 21
preventing rust on tools, 82
to clean vinyl, 21
to prevent screwdriver slipping, 22
to remove ink stains from marble, 38

Chamois,
piano care, 59

Cherry flavored Jell-O,
to touch-up scratches in wood, 39

Cherry wood,
repairing scratches, 48

China cabinet catch,
tip to prevent damage, 27-28

Chocolate,
removing stains from upholstery, 22

Chop sticks, 22

Chrome,
preventing rust, 59

About the Author

Donna Morris has been involved in the restoration of furniture and antiques for more than 30 years. She is a member of the Speaker's Bureau of The Southern California Collector's Association, has guest lectured at California Polytechnic University Pomona, and taught restoration and repairs seminars throughout the Southern California area including special seminars for The Appraisers National Association, The Southern California Collector's Association and The College for Appraisers.

Donna is a contributing author to the I.D.G. book *Antiquing for Dummies* by Ron Zoglin and Deborah Shouse, writes a monthly column entitled *Fixin' Furniture*, and is the author of *More Than 100 Furniture Repairs You Can Do Yourself – A Practical Handbook for Anyone Who Buys, Sells, or Owns Furniture*. Her next book, *Faking It!* is scheduled for release in January 2001. Her books and column evolved from the most frequently asked questions from her clients and students.

She has run a successful restoration business and assisted the Santa Ana School District in restoring the Hiram Clay Kellogg house.

When she is not writing or teaching, Donna spends her free time collecting and repairing antiques and restoring her 1920s Allan Herschell carousel horse.

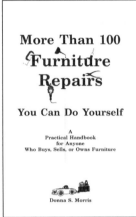

More Than 100
Furniture
Repairs

You Can Do Yourself

A
Practical Handbook
for Anyone
Who Buys, Sells, or Owns Furniture

Donna S. Morris

The best
and
most comprehensive
"How To" book
available!
Without exception.

"This book may well be the bible of furniture repairs, a must have for everyday problems."
  – The Jumble

"The perfect guide ... designed to accommodate everyone from the most inexperienced beginner to the professional refinisher."
  – Victorian Decorating Ideas

"BUY THIS BOOK!! It will pay for itself with only one project."
  – William Price, College for Appraisers

"We highly recommend it to our students and graduates be they novices or professionals. A guide of this nature has been needed for a long time."
  – David Long, Ph. D., CEO/Chancellor, Long University

The *only* book to include:
• repairing antique and contemporary furniture • repairing
wicker and bamboo furniture • repairing outdoor furniture •
weaving new seats • restoring trunks, mirrors ... and practically
every other type of furniture
in one volume!

Order Form

☎ **Telephone Orders:** Call (909) 596-5385

➤ **FAX Orders:** (909) 596-5385

✉ **Postal Orders:** Phoenix Press, Ltd.
1407 Foothill Blvd., #141
La Verne, CA 91750

Please send ____ copies of *More Than 100 Furniture Repairs You Can Do Yourself – A Practical Handbook for Anyone Who Buys, Sells, or Owns Furniture* by Donna S. Morris. ($24.95 per copy, plus shipping and taxes where applicable.)

Please send ____ copies of *Furniture Repairs from A to Z, A Quick Reference Guide of Tips and Techniques* by Donna S. Morris. ($14.95 per copy, plus shipping and taxes where applicable.)

I understand I may return the books for a full refund – for any reason, no questions asked.

Name: _____

Address: _____

City: _____ **State:** _____

Zip Code: _____

Sales Tax: California residents please add 8-1/4%.
Shipping: $2.00 for the first book and 75¢ for each additional book.